EVERYTHING YOUNG ATHLETES NEED TO KNOW

HAYDEN FOX

© Copyright 2025 - All rights reserved.

The content contained within this book may not be reproduced, duplicated or transmitted without direct written permission from the author or the publisher.

Under no circumstances will any blame or legal responsibility be held against the publisher, or author, for any damages, reparation, or monetary loss due to the information contained within this book, either directly or indirectly.

Legal Notice:

This book is copyright protected. It is only for personal use. You cannot amend, distribute, sell, use, quote or paraphrase any part, or the content within this book, without the consent of the author or publisher.

Disclaimer Notice:

Please note the information contained within this document is for educational and entertainment purposes only. All effort has been executed to present accurate, up to date, reliable, complete information. No warranties of any kind are declared or implied. Readers acknowledge that the author is not engaged in the rendering of legal, financial, medical or professional advice. The content within this book has been derived from various sources. Please consult a licensed professional before attempting any techniques outlined in this book.

By reading this document, the reader agrees that under no circumstances is the author responsible for any losses, direct or indirect, that are incurred as a result of the use of the information contained within this document, including, but not limited to, errors, omissions, or inaccuracies.

PARENTS, CLAIM YOUR
FREE GIFTS!

Simply visit

haydenfoxmedia.com

to receive the following:

1000 Conversation Starters
the Whole Family Will Love

100 Fun Screen-Free Activity Ideas
to Enjoy Together as a Family

(You can also scan this QR code)

THIS BOOK BELONGS TO

_____

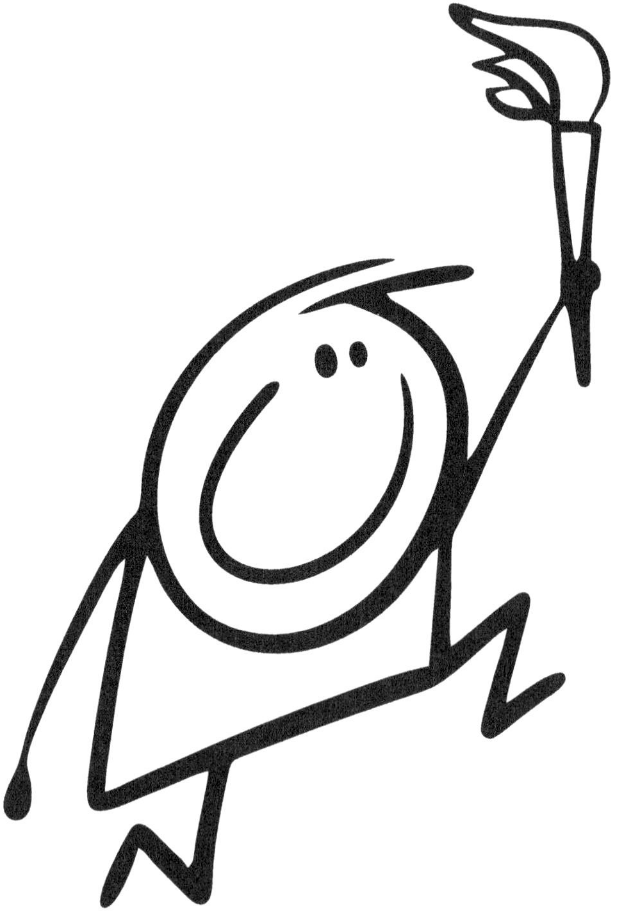

TABLE OF CONTENTS

Introduction 9

Chapter 1: Build a Champion Mindset 12

Chapter 2: Train Like a Champion 24

Chapter 3: Mastering Teamwork
and Leadership 34

Chapter 4: Overcoming Challenges
and Setbacks 44

Chapter 5: The Amazing Power of Consistency ... 54

Chapter 6: Developing Mental Toughness 64

Chapter 7: The Importance of Nutrition 72

Chapter 8: Focus and Concentration 82

Chapter 9: The Art of Strategy and Game IQ 92

Chapter 10: Competition and Rivalries 104

Chapter 11: Building Speed, Agility,
and Strength 112

Chapter 12: Game Day Preparation 124

Conclusion 134

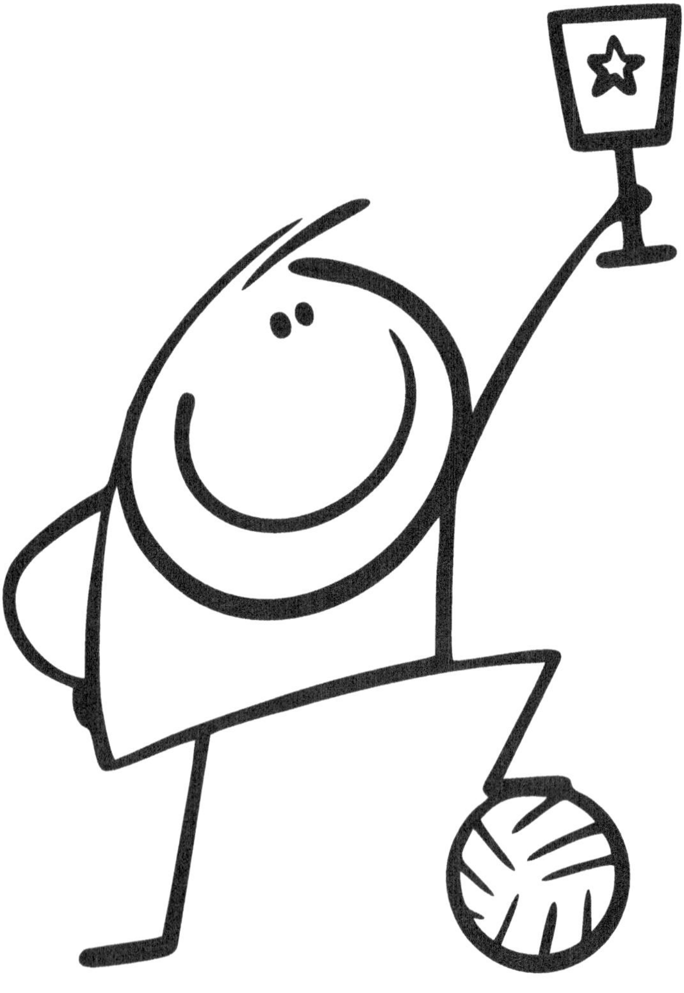

INTRODUCTION

Hey, future superstar!

Ready to take it up a notch? Doesn't matter if you're just starting out or you've been playing forever; this book's got a whole bunch of secret tips and tricks to help you crush it—on the field, on the court or wherever the game takes you.

And look, we all love winning. No question about it. But here's the truth: being a champion isn't just about scoring points or holding up a trophy. It's about learning from every single experience. Winning, losing… even those days when nothing goes right. It's about growing. Getting stronger. Building confidence. Having the mindset that'll get you through the ups and downs, both in sports and in life.

So, what will you gain from this book? Well, here's a quick sneak peek:

- Ever wonder how top athletes keep pushing, even when it gets hard? It's all about mental toughness. You'll need it, too, so we'll dive into how to build it, step by step.

- Want to keep your body in tip-top shape and stay in the game? No more sitting on the sidelines for you.

- Leadership, teamwork—they're not just buzzwords. Want to be the teammate everyone looks to when the pressure's on? You're in the right place.

- Tough game, a case of nerves, bad day? It happens. Every athlete deals with it. But you'll figure out how to face it head-on, and bounce back—every single time.

- There's a lot more where that came from, but let's not spoil everything here.

Now, here's the truth: nobody's perfect, and you don't need to be either. Forget getting it all right the first time. Focus on showing up, putting in the work, and just getting a bit better every day. That's where the magic really happens.

Success is not always easy, and some days will be harder than others; that's just how it goes. But every pro you look up to—every single one of them—started right where you are now. The factor that made them successful is they never quit. They kept pushing through, learning from their mistakes, and showing up. Over and over and over again, until *and* after they became champions.

Now, without further ado, let's get right into it.

Chapter 1
BUILD A CHAMPION MINDSET

What if I told you that your most powerful tool in sports isn't your muscles or your speed, but rather your mind? Yup, you heard right! How you think is the biggest determining factor for success as a young athlete.

When you hear the word "champion," you probably think of someone who wins lots of trophies and medals. But it's a lot more than that; it's about having the right mindset, which then results in acquiring all those trophies and wins—the kind of mindset that allows you to push yourself further and give it your all, no matter how tough things get.

SECRET #1: BELIEVE YOU CAN DO IT

This sounds simple, but I assure you, it's one of the biggest secrets contained within this entire book. When you believe in yourself, you give yourself the best possible chance of success.

Why? Because self-belief enables you to give it all you've got, take chances, and keep going even after making mistakes.

Say you're in the middle of a game and you miss an important shot. It's easy to think, "Ugh, I'm terrible at this." But that won't get you anywhere. So instead, here's a better thought: "Okay, I missed that shot, but it's all right because it's part of my journey in becoming a legend. Let's see how we can make the next one."

Self-belief helps you bounce back and stay focused, no matter the circumstances.

SECRET #2: LEARN FROM EVERY "MISTAKE" OR "FAILURE"

No professional athlete is perfect EVERY single time. Actually, they failed many times before getting to the top. What makes them champions is that they learn from their mistakes instead of letting them bring them down.

So if you fail to score a goal, miss an important pass, or lose a match, ask yourself: "What can I learn from this?" Remember that every mistake is a chance to get better, so instead of feeling bad about it, be inspired.

SECRET #3: PRACTICE POSITIVE SELF-TALK

Did you know you can coach yourself to success? That's right—your inner voice is a powerful tool, so begin to pay attention to what you're telling yourself on a regular basis. Instead of saying, "I'm not good at this," try saying, "I'm still learning this, and with practice, I'll get better. Besides, I'm having a blast!"

Positive self-talk will give you more confidence and help keep you motivated, even when things don't go perfectly. Next time you're feeling nervous before a game, say to yourself, "I've got this! I'm ready to do my best and have lots of fun."

SECRET #4: BREAK DOWN YOUR GOALS

Everyone loves to dream big, but sometimes those dreams seem so unattainable. That's why it's important to break them down into smaller goals that we can accomplish along the way. For example, instead of saying that you'll score 20 points in a game, first aim at scoring 5 points, and then increase it to 10 points after that.

Make every mini goal a stepping stone and use its momentum to carry you on to the next goal!

SECRET #5: YOU CAN'T CONTROL IT ALL

You can't control everything in sports—or in life. Sometimes things are out of our control: teammates having a bad day, our coaches being angry, or the weather not cooperating.

The next time you're going through a challenging situation, remember there are only three things you have control over: your thoughts, your words, and your actions. Focus on bringing your absolute best to these three areas and relax about everything else. Champions know that staying calm and focused, even when things are tough, can turn a game around.

SECRET #6: EMBRACE CHALLENGES

Champions purposely seek out strong opponents and challenges because they know how much better it makes them.

When you find yourself in a challenging situation, rather than thinking about how tough it is, say to yourself, "This is a great opportunity to unfold my potential." The more intense the competition, the better the chance for you to improve. Every problem you encounter makes you that much greater an athlete.

SECRET #7: VISUALIZE YOUR SUCCESS

Did you know that champions often picture victory in their minds right before they play? They do this because it gives them a huge boost of confidence and makes them play better.

Before your next game, try closing your eyes and visualizing yourself making a beautiful pass, scoring a last-minute goal, or running the best-ever race.

Just visualizing these feats in your mind can ease some of the pressure and put you in a victory-focused mindset.

SECRET #8: PERSISTENCE IS KEY

Sports (and life) are not always sunshine and rainbows. You might lose a match, miss your chance at a big win, or be disappointed in yourself over a mistake. The thing that differentiates champions from ordinary people is that they are relentless; they do not stop.

Make it part of your identity not to give up on anything, no matter what. You'll be surprised how far you can get with just that frame of mind alone.

SECRET #9: EFFORT OVER RESULTS

It feels great to win, but what happens when you don't? For most of us, losing can elicit some pretty negative feelings. True champions, however, know that the only thing worth focusing on is what you can control—your effort and attitude. If all you care about is your effort and attitude, you never actually lose. And the scoreboard will reflect that, too!

SECRET #10: PRACTICE GRATITUDE

Being a good athlete is actually not about winning at all; it's about enjoying the process. Always be grateful for the chance to play, for your teammates, and for the opportunity to grow as an athlete and as a person. If you dwell on the things you're thankful for, it will keep your mind positive and your heart open, which enables you to play better.

SECRET #11: LOVE THE PROCESS

Success is a process, and it takes time. Becoming a great athlete is also a process. Don't get too caught up in the end goal; instead, enjoy the process of learning, practicing, and getting better along the way.

SECRET #12: BE YOUR OWN BIGGEST CHEERLEADER

It's nice when others cheer you on, but how you motivate yourself is what matters most. Make a big deal out of your small steps forward, because when you believe in yourself, you keep going.

SECRET #13: KEEP A "CHAMPION JOURNAL"

Try journaling about your goals, challenges, and victories; putting your thoughts down on paper will help you to reflect on how much you've grown—which is a great way to set yourself up for massive success.

SECRET #14: SURROUND YOURSELF WITH POSITIVE PEOPLE

Surround yourself with good people who have a positive influence on you. Hang out with teammates, friends, and coaches who lift you up and believe in you. Positivity keeps you motivated and focused.

SECRET #15: STAY CURIOUS

Ask questions and be curious. Winners are always looking at ways they can improve and understand the game better. Whether it's watching how the pros play or asking your coach for advice, be curious and eager to learn.

With these 15 secrets, you're already on your way to building the kind of mindset that helps champions succeed. Now that you've got your mind in the game, let's dive into the next chapter and start working on your skills!

Chapter 2
TRAIN LIKE A CHAMPION

Now that you've got the right mindset, let's talk about training. No one becomes a great athlete overnight; it requires a lot of hard work and practice in building up one's skills and strength. Let's go through a few secrets that will help you train more effectively with each passing day.

SECRET #16: PRACTICE WITH PURPOSE

Practice is great, but if you really want to get better, you have to practice with purpose—meaning, work on something specific you want to improve, whether that's footwork, shooting, passing, or whatever.

Instead of just going through the motions, set a small goal for each practice. For example, if you're working on dribbling, make a goal to do 10 perfect dribbles in a row. Practicing with purpose makes every session count.

SECRET #17: MASTER THE BASICS

The best in the world make time to work on the basics, whatever that may be for their sport. Mastering the basics are a must if you want to achieve massive success as an athlete.

Don't worry if it feels a bit tedious at times, especially at first; everything else becomes way easier once you get this down.

SECRET #18: TRAIN BOTH SIDES OF YOUR BODY

This doesn't apply to every sport, but for the ones it does apply to, it's worth noting. You might be really good at kicking or throwing with one side, but to be a well-rounded athlete, you need to work on your non-dominant side too. For example, if you usually shoot with your right foot, spend some time practicing with your left.

Training both sides makes you a more versatile and unpredictable player.

SECRET #19: FOCUS ON YOUR FOOTWORK

Footwork is among the most basic skills in almost every sport: be it soccer, basketball, or tennis, good footwork will make you faster, more agile, and more effective.

Spend time on drills that improve your speed and coordination, like ladder drills or quick sprints. The better your footwork, the faster you'll be able to react during a game.

SECRET #20: BE CONSISTENT

Consistency is the magic ingredient in both sports and life that will carry you towards success. You don't need to practice for hours on end, but make sure to do something every single day. Even as little as 20-30 minutes of daily, focused practice is going to make a huge difference over time.

Create a routine and follow it. Winners are built from what they do consistently when no one is watching.

SECRET #21: REST AND RECOVERY ARE KEY

Hard work is important, but so is rest. Your body needs a little time to recover after tough workouts and games. Plus, rest days actually prevent injuries and help your muscles get stronger.

Get enough sleep, drink plenty of water, and take days off when your body tells you to.

SECRET #22: STRETCH TO STAY STRONG

Another important aspect of training like a champion is stretching. It keeps your muscles flexible and aids in the prevention of injuries. Maybe even more importantly, though, stretching after each practice or workout helps your body wind down and recover.

Try adding a few minutes of stretching to your routine, focusing on the muscles you use the most in your sport.

SECRET #23: MIX IT UP WITH CROSS-TRAINING

Cross-training simply means training in activities other than the one representing your sport. For example, a soccer player can build up their endurance through swimming or biking, while a basketball player could develop better balance and flexibility by doing yoga.

It keeps you in shape and works different muscles. Plus, it's fun to try out something different once in a while!

SECRET #24: FUEL YOUR BODY LIKE A PRO

What you eat is just as important as how you train. Healthy and nutritious foods fuel the body and enable it to put up the best performance possible. Try to eat a balanced diet that includes fruits and vegetables, lean proteins, and whole grains.

And don't forget to drink plenty of water—proper hydration keeps your muscles working smoothly and will help you avoid cramping and fatigue during games.

SECRET #25: TRACK YOUR PROGRESS

How do you know if you're getting any better? By tracking your progress! Keep a training log and note down what you're training on, what went well, and what you want to improve.

Doing this is going to keep you motivated and let you look back and see how far you've come. Additionally, it will give you a chance to celebrate your improvements, no matter how small they are.

SECRET #26: WARM UP BEFORE EVERY PRACTICE

You should always warm up your muscles to get them ready for action and prevent injuries. Do some light exercises or stretching for a few minutes before getting into whatever physical activity you're doing. This will have your body at peak performance right off the bat.

SECRET #27: COOL DOWN AFTER EVERY PRACTICE

In the same vein as the previous secret, it's important to cool down after practices. Perform a few minutes of light stretching or slow exercises to help your body recover and ease muscle soreness.

SECRET #28: CHALLENGE YOURSELF WITH NEW DRILLS

You have to push your limits if you want to keep getting better. Try adding new drills to your training regimen that address different skills. The more challenges you throw at yourself, the more you'll grow as an athlete.

SECRET #29: TRAIN YOUR MIND TOO

As we know from Chapter 1, training isn't just physical—it's mental too. Spend a few minutes each day doing mental exercises like focusing on your breathing, visualizing success, or practicing mindfulness to stay sharp and focused.

SECRET #30: TRAIN WITH FRIENDS

Training with friends who are as dedicated as you is a great way to get better faster; they may have tips and tricks that you don't know about (and vice versa). And obviously, it's more fun too!

Chapter 3
MASTERING TEAMWORK AND LEADERSHIP

Being a great athlete isn't just about what you can do on your own—it's also about how well you work with your team. Learning how to be a good teammate and leader will truly make a difference in your success if you're playing any type of team sport. Here are some secrets to help you master teamwork and become a strong leader both on and off the field.

SECRET #31: COMMUNICATION IS KEY

The most important part of being a great teammate is learning how to communicate. This means not only talking with your teammates during the game, calling for the ball, directions, or anything else that might be needed, but also listening to what your teammates and coach are saying.

Good communication helps things run smoothly within the team and ensures everyone is on the same page.

SECRET #32: PUT THE TEAM FIRST

It is natural to want to be that star player, but in team sports, it's all about keeping your focus on the team. Sometimes you have to make the pass for the good of the group, even if it means less of a spotlight on you.

Doing what's best for the team (not just what's best for you) makes you a good teammate.

SECRET #33: BE A ROLE MODEL

Leadership is not about being the loudest or most dominant player; it's about setting a good example for others. Show your teammates how to work hard, stay positive, and give your best effort.

Lead by example and others will follow you. You'll achieve much more together as a team.

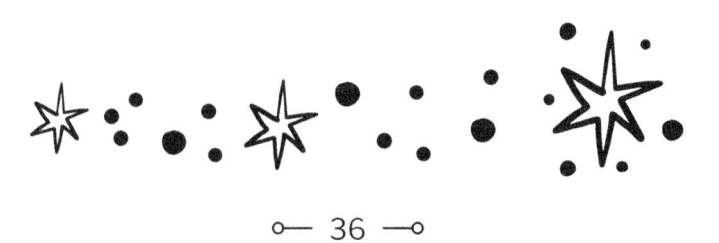

SECRET #34: BUILD TRUST WITH YOUR TEAM

Trust is the cement that holds a team together. To develop trust, always be dependable. Make it to practices, keep your commitments, and give each game your all.

When your teammates know they can count on you, the team is stronger.

SECRET #35: STAY POSITIVE

Games don't always go as planned, but a good teammate stays positive and keeps their head up, even in the toughest of times. It's really easy to get frustrated or upset when things aren't going well, but letting those feelings get the best of you won't help anyone.

Being positive also increases your team's confidence and keeps them motivated to make an epic comeback.

SECRET #36: CELEBRATE YOUR TEAMMATES' SUCCESSES

A great athlete knows how to celebrate others. When your teammate makes an awesome play or scores a goal, be the first to cheer them on. Showing your support boosts team spirit and helps everyone feel valued.

SECRET #37: LEARN TO GIVE (AND TAKE) CONSTRUCTIVE CRITICISM

Constructive criticism is advice that helps you improve, but it's not always easy to hear. A good teammate is able to give constructive feedback in a helpful way, while also remaining open to receiving it. If a teammate is telling you how to do something better, just listen and thank them for the input. And if you want to give some feedback, do so in a nice way, focusing on how your teammate can improve.

SECRET #38: PLAY YOUR ROLE

You must understand how to play your position on the team. Maybe you play as a defender in soccer, or perhaps you're a point guard in basketball, or a forward in hockey—whatever your position, just make sure that you become the best at playing that position.

If each member is doing their job correctly, then the team is a well-oiled machine.

SECRET #39: BE COOL UNDER PRESSURE

Games can get intense, and sometimes things can get overwhelming for certain teammates. A good leader knows how to keep calm and focused when the situation demands it, even when pressure is at an all-time high. By keeping your cool, you not only help yourself play better, but also help the rest of your team keep their focus.

SECRET #40: ENCOURAGE AND SUPPORT YOUR TEAMMATES

Everyone has bad days, and sometimes your teammates might feel down. As a leader, part of your job is to encourage and support them, offering a few kind words while reminding them of their strengths. Help get them back in the game. If your teammates feel supported, they'll want to put their best foot forward.

SECRET #41: BE COACHABLE

Being coachable means being open to feedback from your coach or teammates and willing to improve. A great leader understands that they don't know everything and is always ready to learn more. Listen to advice and take it seriously—doing so will make you a better athlete and teammate.

SECRET #42: ENERGIZE YOUR TEAM

The team will sometimes need a little more energy. Whether you give high-fives, a quick pep talk, or just a spurt of genuine enthusiasm, be that person who keeps the energy of the team high. If everyone is fired up, they're going to do their best work.

GO TEAM!

SECRET #43: KNOW WHEN TO STEP UP AND WHEN TO STEP BACK

A good leader knows when to step up and take the reins, but also when to step back and allow others to shine. There will be times when your team needs you to lead, and other times when someone else's strengths can carry the team forward. Learning how to balance both is what makes a great teammate and leader.

SECRET #44: KEEP THINGS FUN

Sports are hard work, but they're supposed to be fun as well. As a leader, try to keep things light and enjoyable. Have fun together as teammates and joke around about tough situations; remind each other that in the end, it's about playing the game and having tons of fun, win or lose.

SECRET #45: BE HUMBLE

Be humble when you make a great play. Great leaders don't brag about themselves or put others down.

Now that you have all these secrets on how to be an awesome teammate and leader, it's time to put them into practice! Remember, every great team is built on trust, communication, and support. Whether you're leading the charge or just playing your role, these tips are going to help you make your team even stronger and more successful.

Chapter 4
OVERCOMING CHALLENGES AND SETBACKS

Every athlete goes through hard times, be it losses, facing a challenging opponent, or even sustaining an injury—but this is where champions differentiate themselves from everyone else; they learn how to move past setbacks and turn those challenges into stepping stones. Let's dive into some simple strategies that'll help you power through any obstacle.

SECRET #46: FOCUS ON WHAT YOU CAN DO BETTER

Instead of worrying about the things you have no control over, worry about how you can better your craft. Whether you're working on footwork, stamina, or game strategy, there's always something that can be improved, especially right after a tough game or practice.

SECRET #47: DEVELOP A PRE-GAME RITUAL

Create a ritual that places you in the right frame of mind before each game or practice. It could be listening to your favorite music, doing deep breathing, or just visualizing success. This will help calm your nerves and build confidence.

SECRET #48: TURN STRESS INTO POWER

Pressure is part of every competitive sport, but you can use it to your advantage. Instead of letting stress overwhelm you, channel that energy into pure power and focus. Use the adrenaline rush to sharpen your concentration and abilities to superhero-like levels!

SECRET #49: PRACTICE MENTAL RECOVERY AFTER SETBACKS

Just like your body needs time to recover, your mind does too. Therefore, if you experience a tough loss or feel frustrated over a mistake, take time to recover mentally. Go over what happened, but don't stay there too long. Give yourself some time off from the mental strain to come back even stronger.

SECRET #50: USE SETBACKS TO BUILD RESILIENCE

Never forget that each setback you face is a chance to grow tougher. Resilience isn't just about pushing through—it's about learning to bounce back quickly. After every challenge, remind yourself, "This is making me stronger."

SECRET #51: REFRAME NEGATIVE THOUGHTS

When you're frustrated or disappointed, negative thoughts can sneak in. Learn to reframe them into something positive. For example, if you think, "I'll never get this right," reframe it to, "I'm still learning, and every practice gets me closer to my goal."

SECRET #52: CELEBRATE PROGRESS, NOT PERFECTION

Instead of aiming for perfection, focus on the progress you've made and how far you've come. Whether it's improving your speed by just a little or getting better at a certain skill, those small wins are what matter most.

SECRET #53: BREAK DOWN BIG CHALLENGES

When something seems hard, try breaking it down into smaller steps. If you have a big game coming up, for example, start by focusing on specific drills to master during practice, then build up to an overall game strategy.

SECRET #54: BE FLEXIBLE WITH YOUR GOALS

Goal setting is important, but at the same time, you need to be willing to adapt those goals. You may sometimes need to revise your goals in view of new challenges or situations that arise. Being open to change will make you adaptable and successful no matter what comes along.

SECRET #55: USE VISUALIZATION FOR RECOVERY

If you've sustained an injury or some other form of setback, just think about how you're going to become stronger and better through this experience. This not only helps you feel better—it might even speed up your recovery!

SECRET #56: KEEP A "CHALLENGE JOURNAL"

Just like you track your wins, keep a journal of the challenges you've faced and how you overcame them. Writing down your struggles and victories will help you see your progress and remind you of how resilient you are.

SECRET #57: FIND STRENGTH IN TEAM SUPPORT

When things get tough, lean on your teammates. Remember, you're never alone; your team is with you all the way. Whether it's sharing advice or just giving each other a pep talk, team support makes challenges easier to handle.

SECRET #58: STAY ACTIVE DURING RECOVERY

If you're injured, don't sit around feeling stuck or lazy. Find ways to stay active without aggravating your injury. You can work on other areas of your body, practice your mental game, or learn more about game tactics. Staying active during recovery keeps your mind sharp and your body ready for when you return.

SECRET #59: CREATE A POST-GAME REFLECTION HABIT

After every game or practice, take a few minutes to reflect on what went well and what didn't. Use this reflection time to think about how you handled challenges and what you can improve for next time. This habit will help you continue to grow after every game.

SECRET #60: BUILD CONFIDENCE FROM EVERY SETBACK

Confidence doesn't just come from winning—you can also gain confidence through overcoming challenges. The more often you get through tough situations, the more unshakeable your confidence becomes. Use your setbacks as fuel to strengthen your belief in yourself.

With these secrets under your belt, you'll be ready for whatever comes your way. It's not about preventing or worrying about setbacks; it's about learning to overcome them and change how you see them. The more challenges you encounter, the more robust you become!

Chapter 5
THE AMAZING POWER OF CONSISTENCY

Great athletes are not defined by a single performance but by the little things they do daily. All the little things that you do, from keeping up with practice to building good habits, compound over time. Let's get into how you can develop winning habits that keep you moving consistently toward becoming a champion.

SECRET #61: START SMALL, BUILD BIG

Big changes don't happen overnight. If you're not comfortable making a big change to your routine, start with a small habit and build from that. Whether it's adding 5 minutes of stretching per day or incorporating another drill into your practice, the small changes will lead to big improvements over time.

SECRET #62: DEVELOP A DAILY ROUTINE

Having a routine keeps you focused because you know that you're always working toward your goals. Create a simple daily schedule allowing for practice time, rest, and healthy habits like stretching and hydrating. The more consistent you are, the easier it is to stick to your routine in the long term.

SECRET #63: THE POWER OF REPETITION

Repetition is what separates the good from the great, especially when perfecting a skill. Whatever you're practicing—footwork, shooting, passing, etc.—the more you do it, the better you'll get. Keep running through each drill until it becomes second nature. It should become so natural that your body is able to do it without thinking.

SECRET #64: FOCUS ON CONSISTENCY, NOT PERFECTION

It's easy to get frustrated when things aren't going perfectly. But champions understand something: it's not about perfection—it's about consistency. Show up to every practice, even when you don't feel your best. That's the only way you'll ever make real progress.

SECRET #65: SOMETHING IS BETTER THAN NOTHING

Even if you're feeling really tired or you're not having the best day, show up and do at least a little bit of practice. Something is always infinitely better than nothing.

SECRET #66: CREATE A SCHEDULE

One of the best ways to make sure you keep up with your practice is to create a schedule. A schedule makes you much more likely to stay on track. A great way to do this is to split up the day into 1-hour or half-hour blocks and schedule the important things that you need to do in those time blocks.

SECRET #67: HAVE AN ACCOUNTABILITY PARTNER

An accountability partner is someone who makes sure that you're doing what you said you would. Sometimes we get lazy and don't follow up on our plans, but an accountability partner is there to hold you accountable. This person can be anyone who sees you often or is always in contact with you, such as a parent, best friend, or sibling.

SECRET #68: HAVE SMALLER SESSIONS

Instead of having one or two long, tiring practice sessions, break those up into multiple shorter ones. This can be both less tiring and more impactful.

SECRET #69: SURROUND YOURSELF WITH GOOD HABITS

Your environment matters when it comes to building habits, so surround yourself with teammates, coaches, and friends who encourage good habits. Being around people who are focused on improvement will inspire you to stay consistent too.

SECRET #70: STICK TO A HEALTHY SLEEP SCHEDULE

Getting enough sleep is crucial to ensure you're performing at your best. Set a regular bedtime and make sure you get 8-10 hours of sleep each night; this helps your body recover and keeps your mind sharp for each new day of training.

SECRET #71: PRACTICE UNDER PRESSURE

It's all well and good to practice when everything is relaxed, but in actual games, you're going to have pressure on you. So, in your practice, try to replicate those high-pressure moments. For example, you can pretend it's the last minute of the game and you have to make a game-winning shot. The more you practice under pressure, the calmer you'll be when it really counts because you'll be used to that feeling.

SECRET #72: FOCUS ON THE FUN

When we really want something (like improving our skills), we tend to get attached to that outcome. That's fine, but never, ever forget that the reason you're playing this sport is because you find it fun and enjoyable. If you're ever feeling tired or unexcited about practice because you've been so focused on improving, shift your focus to the feeling of fun and watch how quickly your mood changes!

Remember to have fun!

SECRET #73: USE AFFIRMATIONS AS PART OF YOUR ROUTINE

Here's another powerful tool that should be part of your daily ritual. Before going to bed and when you wake up in the morning, or whenever you have a spare moment, repeat a phrase that makes you feel good—for example, "I am so energized and strong. I can take on the world right now. I am ready to give it my all, and that's what counts." Affirmations keep your mind focused on positivity and primed for success.

SECRET #74: FUEL YOUR BODY CONSISTENTLY

Just as you train regularly, your body needs to be fueled regularly with the right foods. Eat plenty of well-balanced meals that will give you the energy to train and perform at the highest possible level. The right fuel makes quite a difference in how you feel and play.

SECRET #75: PLAY THE LONG GAME

Success does not come overnight. It takes time to build strong habits that bring long-term results. Just embrace the journey and remind yourself every day: every time you practice, every time you stick to your habits, you're one step closer to your goals.

When you implement these secrets, you'll be equipped to consistently build powerful habits that will lead you to success. Remember, a champion is not made in one game; it's their daily habits that make them great. Just show up, be patient, and trust the process—you've got this!

Chapter 6
DEVELOPING MENTAL TOUGHNESS

When it comes to sports, your mental game is just as important as your physical one. Mental toughness allows you to push through challenges (even when things get really tough) and stay focused under pressure. Let's dive into some secrets that will help you build the kind of mental toughness champions are made of.

SECRET #76: UNDERSTAND WHAT MENTAL TOUGHNESS REALLY MEANS

Being mentally tough does not mean being tough all the time; it means being able to face whatever comes your way—be it a tough opponent, bad call from the referee, or even inner doubts. This means keeping calm and focused, even when things aren't going your way. With mental toughness, you are in control of your emotions; you stay in the moment and find a way to keep moving forward, no matter what happens, instead of becoming frustrated or discouraged.

Mental toughness also includes resilience: the ability to move on from any failure, loss, or mistake. It doesn't mean ignoring the setbacks; it's actually the opposite. Being resilient means embracing the fact that setbacks don't define you—rather, you emerge from each challenge stronger, both physically and mentally.

SECRET #77: PRACTICE STAYING CALM UNDER PRESSURE

The best athletes know how to stay calm when the pressure's on. Whether it's a big game, a championship match, or simply a high-stakes moment, learning to keep your nerves in check is important.

One good way of keeping calm under pressure is focusing on your breathing.

Whenever you start to feel nervous or overwhelmed, breathe in deeply for a count of four, hold your breath for a count of four, and exhale for a count of four. This little breathing trick will soothe you, relax your body, and calm your mind to focus on your performance.

Another thing that will help you stay calm is focusing on what you can control. You can't always control the result of a game, the weather, or an opponent's move. What you can always control is your effort, mindset, and attitude. When you put the focus on those things, you'll experience relief from the pressure of everything else.

SECRET #78: BUILD CONFIDENCE THROUGH PREPARATION

The best way to build up confidence is to be prepared. If you walk into a game or practice and feel well-prepared, you're going to have more confidence in your ability to do your job. You can prepare by putting in the work during practice, mastering your skills, and knowing your game plan inside and out.

Preparation is not only about the physical part; it's about mental preparation, too. Visualize yourself in different scenarios, like hitting a game-winning shot or keeping your focus after a mistake. If you have prepared mentally for a variety of scenarios, then when the time comes, you'll feel a lot more confident in your ability to handle them.

SECRET #79: THINK POSITIVE

Your mind is a powerful tool, and what you think about may make all the difference in how well you perform. Positive thinking means believing in your abilities and focusing on the things you're doing well. If you focus on what's going right, you're very likely to be in a flow state and stay motivated.

You can also practice positive thinking by coming up with a list of positive affirmations like the ones we talked about before.

SECRET #80: MANAGE YOUR EMOTIONS

Sports can be an emotional rollercoaster: high highs when you're winning, low lows when things aren't going your way. A big part of dealing with that is mental toughness—learning how to handle your emotions. It's natural to feel frustrated when you lose or excited when you win, but champions know how to keep those things at bay.

So, when you're getting worked up, stop and check in with yourself for a second: "How am I feeling right now? What can I do to keep myself centered and focused?" This approach keeps you in touch with how you're feeling but won't let the feelings consume you. By keeping a handle on your emotions, you'll be able to make better decisions out there on the field and focus on what really counts: giving it your best shot.

SECRET #81: CHALLENGES ARE FUN

It's easy to get discouraged or overwhelmed when facing a tough opponent or another type of adversity—but mental toughness will turn those challenges into opportunities. Instead of seeing a tough situation as a problem, try to see it as a fun challenge that you can't wait to tackle. That's a huge difference in mindset. Think of hard situations as super fun opportunities to better yourself, and you'll be surprised at how quickly you improve as an athlete.

SECRET #82: STAY FOCUSED ON THE PRESENT MOMENT

One of the best ways to build mental toughness is to stay focused on the present. It's so easy to get caught up in worries about the future, like whether or not you're going to win, or thoughts about past mistakes.

But champions know how to stay focused on what's happening right now. In the middle of a game, or even practice, keep your focus on what's in front of you. Not what's going to happen next, not what happened before—just be in the present moment. That focus keeps you calm and playing your best.

Chapter 7
THE IMPORTANCE OF NUTRITION

What you eat and drink can make a huge difference in your performance as an athlete. Your body is like a car; if you don't give it the right fuel, it won't perform as it should. Knowing how to fuel your body properly through good nutrition and hydration will aid in top performance, faster recovery, and feeling good both on and off the field.

SECRET #83: BALANCED NUTRITION

A healthy body is one in which there is a balanced intake of food. A balanced meal includes proteins to help the body build and repair muscles, carbohydrates (such as whole grains, fruits, and vegetables) to supply the energy needed to get through practices and games, and good fats (like avocados, nuts, and olive oil) to keep the body running right. Eat whole (meaning not processed), nutritious foods that keep you feeling strong and ready to play.

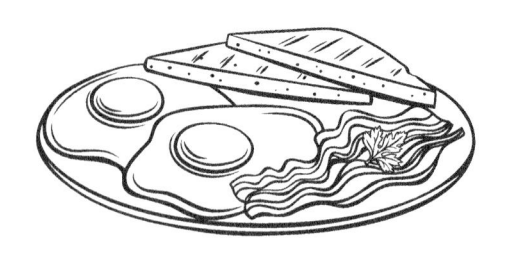

SECRET #84: DON'T SKIP BREAKFAST

Many people say that breakfast is the most important meal of the day, and for athletes, that couldn't be more accurate. After sleeping all night, your body needs to recharge with a healthy breakfast to get your day going energetically. Skipping breakfast will make you feel quite tired and less focused, which may affect your performance in practice or games.

A good breakfast for athletes should have a balance of carbohydrates, protein, and healthy fats, as we talked about in the previous secret. For example, oatmeal with fruit and nuts, scrambled eggs with whole-grain toast, or a yogurt, spinach, and berry smoothie—all these are very good choices that will give you lots of energy to tackle the day.

SECRET #85: HYDRATE, HYDRATE, HYDRATE!

One of the best things you can do for your body is hydrate. When you're being active, you lose water through your sweat; if you don't replace it, you'll begin to feel tired, dizzy, and sluggish. You need to drink water throughout the day, specifically before, during, and after practices, to keep your body running smoothly.

SECRET #86: TIME YOUR SNACKS AND MEALS FOR PEAK PERFORMANCE

When you eat is just as important as what you eat. You want to time your meals and snacks correctly in relation to practices and games to perform at your best. Make sure you eat a meal about 2-3 hours before a game or practice. This allows time for your body to digest and use the energy from the food for the activity ahead.

If you need a boost just before practice, have a snack, like a banana, a handful of nuts, or a granola bar. Right after every practice and game, you definitely need to refuel with a meal that includes protein and carbohydrates to help your muscles recover and replenish energy stores. You might have something like grilled chicken with rice and mixed veggies or a turkey sandwich on whole-grain bread.

SECRET #87: DON'T FORGET ABOUT HEALTHY FATS

When you think about healthy eating, fats might not be the first thing that pop into your head, but they actually are very important to your diet. Healthy fats help your body absorb vitamins and provide you with sustained energy. Add foods such as avocados, nuts, seeds, and olive oil to your snacks and meals to get the benefits of these healthy fats.

SECRET #88: SNACK SMART

Snacking is a great way to ensure you're your energy levels are stable all day. Be very cautious, however, about what you snack on. Rather than chips or candy, look for a snack that gives you energy that will last for a longer period and support your training.

Healthy athlete snacking options include yogurt and fruit, peanut butter on whole-grain crackers, trail mix with nuts and dried fruit, and veggies with hummus. Snacking smart will help you avoid energy crashes and keep you fueled for practices and games. Pack healthy snacks in your bag so that when hunger strikes, you're always prepared.

SECRET #89: EAT ENOUGH TO SUPPORT YOUR TRAINING

As an athlete, your body tends to burn many more calories than a person who's less active. That means you have to eat accordingly, matching the calories to your training. Otherwise, you'll likely start feeling lethargic and weak, or possibly have difficulty focusing during games.

Listen to the hunger signals in your body; make sure you eat enough to meet your energy needs. This doesn't mean you should stuff yourself with food, but you do need to properly nourish your body, especially on heavy training days. Eat a well-balanced meal with plenty of nutrients to keep your energy up and your body strong.

SECRET #90: USE SMOOTHIES TO PACK IN NUTRIENTS

Smoothies are the best way to condense a lot of nutrients into one easy-to-make meal or snack. Try blending fruits, veggies, yogurt, protein powder, and healthy fats like avocado or nuts for a genuinely tasty and nutritious drink. These are great for a quick breakfast or post-practice recovery snack.

One tasty recipe is to blend a banana, spinach, a scoop of protein powder, and almond milk to make a smoothie full of energy, protein, and nutrients. Smoothies are also a great way to sneak in extra vegetables, such as spinach or kale, and not even taste them!

SECRET #91: AVOID SUGARY DRINKS AND JUNK FOOD

Sugary drinks, such as soda and energy beverages, will give you a boost, but it will never last. You'll crash and feel even more tired later on. Stick to water or milk, or turn to natural fruit juices to keep your energy levels sustained. The same goes for junk foods like chips, candy, and fast food. These foods will not give your body the nourishment that it needs to put its best foot forward. Try to keep these treats to a minimum and focus on whole, nutrient-rich foods that will energize your body, enabling greater success.

With these secrets, you've learned how to properly fuel your body and stay hydrated, setting yourself up for success in your sport. Remember, what you eat and drink has a big impact on how you feel and perform, so make healthy choices that will help you be the best athlete you can be!

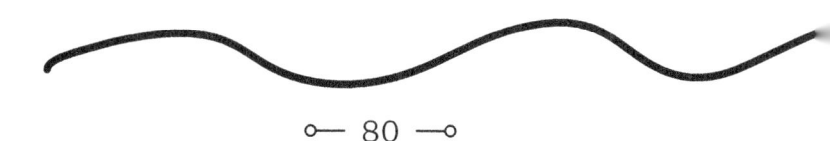

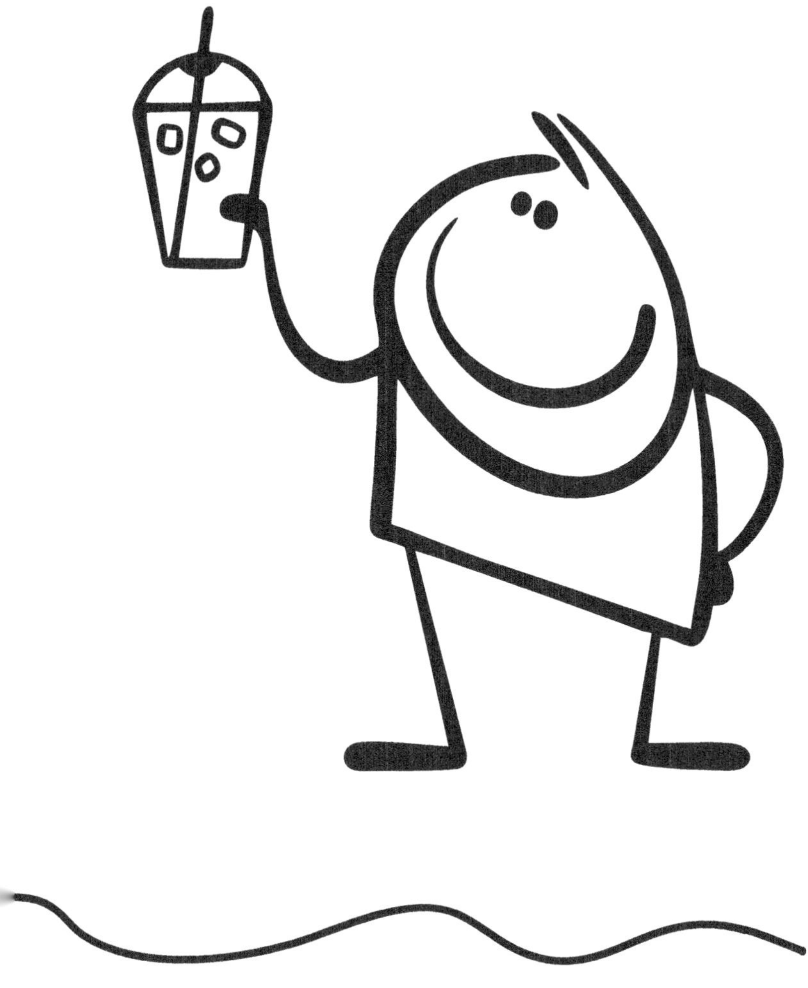

Chapter 8
FOCUS AND CONCENTRATION

Focus is one of the most important skills in sports. It's the ability to shut out distractions, stay in the moment, and give your best effort on every play. But focus doesn't just happen—it's a skill you can develop and strengthen over time. In this chapter, we'll explore powerful secrets to help you master focus and concentration so you can stay locked in, no matter what's happening around you.

SECRET #92: FOCUS ON ONE THING AT A TIME

One of the biggest mistakes athletes make is trying to think about too many things at once. When you focus on multiple things—like what the score is, what the coach is saying, and how your teammates are performing—it's easy to lose track of what you're supposed to be doing. To improve your concentration, practice focusing on just one thing at a time.

For example, during a game, your one focus might be getting into the right position on defense. In practice, it could be perfecting your technique on a specific drill. By zeroing in on one task at a time, you'll be more effective and less overwhelmed. It takes discipline to keep your mind from jumping around, but the more you practice focusing on one thing, the sharper your concentration will become.

SECRET #93: TRAIN YOUR BRAIN WITH MENTAL EXERCISES

Your brain is like a muscle, and just like your body, it needs exercise to stay strong. One of the best ways to sharpen your focus is to do mental exercises that challenge your concentration. A simple one is to sit quietly and focus on your breathing for five minutes, trying not to let your mind wander. If it does, just gently bring your attention back to your breath.

You can also play games that require concentration, like puzzles or memory games, to improve your mental agility. The goal is to train your brain to stay focused for longer periods of time, even when there are distractions. By practicing these exercises regularly, you'll notice that you're able to concentrate more easily, both in sports and in other areas of your life.

SECRET #94: CREATE A FOCUS ROUTINE

Having a routine before games and practices can help get your mind into focus mode. A focus routine is a series of actions or steps that you do every time to prepare yourself mentally. It could be as simple as taking a few deep breaths, repeating a positive affirmation, and doing a quick stretch.

The routine acts like a switch for your brain, signaling that it's time to focus and block out distractions. Over time, this routine becomes automatic, and you'll find that you're able to get into the zone more quickly and easily. Find what works best for you—whether it's listening to a specific song, visualizing success, or doing a few calming exercises. The key is consistency.

SECRET #95: BREAK GAMES INTO SMALLER MOMENTS

Thinking about a whole game at once can feel overwhelming. To stay focused, try breaking it down into smaller, more manageable moments. Instead of thinking about the whole game, focus on the next five minutes or the next play. By breaking the game down, you give your mind a clear, smaller task to focus on, which helps reduce stress and keeps you engaged.

This technique also works in practice. If you're working on a difficult skill, instead of thinking about mastering the entire drill, focus on nailing the first few reps. Once you've done that, move on to the next set. This approach keeps you in the present and prevents your mind from wandering to the end result.

SECRET #96: STAY FLEXIBLE IN YOUR FOCUS

Being focused doesn't necessarily mean concentrating on one thing for the entire game. In fact, great athletes learn how to shift their focus depending on what's happening in the moment. For example, during a game, you might need to switch your focus from your positioning on the field, to your opponent, to your own movements—all within a few seconds.

Staying flexible with your focus means knowing when to zoom in on the details (like dribbling the ball past a defender) and when to zoom out to see the bigger picture (like finding the best teammate to pass to). Practice switching your focus between narrow tasks and broader game awareness. This flexibility will help you adapt to changing situations quickly and make smart decisions under pressure.

SECRET #97: PRACTICE MINDFULNESS ON THE FIELD

Mindfulness is the practice of staying in the moment, without getting caught up in thoughts about the past or future. In sports, this means focusing on the task at hand, whether it's making a pass, running a play, or defending your opponent, without worrying about what just happened or what's coming next.

To practice mindfulness during a game, focus all of your attention on your body and how it feels in the moment. Notice how your feet move, how your muscles react, and how your breath flows. By staying present, you'll be able to react more quickly and make better decisions. Practicing mindfulness regularly, both on and off the field, will train your brain to stay focused when it matters most.

SECRET #98: MANAGE YOUR ENERGY LEVELS

Focus isn't just determined by your mental state—it's also greatly impacted by how well you manage your energy levels. If you're exhausted, it's much harder to concentrate. That's why it's important to pay attention to how you're feeling physically and take steps to maintain your energy throughout the day.

This means getting enough sleep, eating nutritious meals, and staying hydrated so that your body and mind are ready to focus when it's game time. During practice or games, take short breaks to recharge if needed. Even a quick stretch or a sip of water can refresh your energy and bring your focus back to where it needs to be.

SECRET #99: EMBRACE THE FLOW STATE

The flow state, often called "being in the zone," is when you're so focused on what you're doing that everything else seems to disappear. In this state, your movements feel effortless, your mind is clear, and you're fully engaged in the task at hand. Athletes who learn how to reach this state regularly are often the ones who perform at the highest level.

To enter a state of flow, focus on the joy of playing the game rather than the outcome. When you let go of the pressure to win or perform perfectly and simply immerse yourself in the moment, you're more likely to reach that state of peak concentration. The more you practice this, the more often you'll find yourself in the flow during games and practices.

Implementing these secrets will help you develop the focus and concentration you need to perform at your best in every game and practice. Remember, focus is a skill—a habit that you build over time. By mastering the art of concentration, you'll find yourself making better decisions, staying calm under pressure, and playing with confidence.

Chapter 9
THE ART OF STRATEGY AND GAME IQ

Success in sports isn't just about being fast or strong—it's also about being smart. Knowing how to think strategically during a game can give you the edge you need to outsmart your opponents and make the best decisions in the heat of the moment. This chapter will teach you how to improve your game IQ and think like a champion.

SECRET #100: UNDERSTAND THE BIG PICTURE

Every sport has a "big picture," meaning the overall goal or strategy for your team. In soccer, for example, the big picture might be maintaining possession of the ball and controlling the pace of the game. In basketball, it might be creating open shots by spacing the floor and passing quickly.

To improve your game IQ, start by understanding the big picture of your sport. Pay attention to how the game flows and how different strategies come into play. Watch professional or college games and notice the tactics teams use to control the game. The more you understand the big picture, the better you'll be at seeing how each play fits into the overall strategy.

SECRET #101: LEARN TO READ THE OPPONENT

One of the best ways to outsmart your opponents is by learning to read their movements and predict what they'll do next. This skill, called "anticipation," is what separates good players from great ones. During a game, pay close attention to your opponent's body language, positioning, and tendencies. Are they favoring a particular side? Do they always dribble with their right hand? Do they hesitate before taking a shot?

Picking up on these small details lets you anticipate their next move and adjust your strategy accordingly. This might mean positioning yourself better to intercept a pass, closing off their strong side, or preparing to block their shot. Anticipation gives you a split-second advantage, which can make all the difference in a game.

SECRET #102: ADJUST YOUR STRATEGY DURING THE GAME

Even the best game plans don't always work perfectly, and part of having great game IQ is knowing when and how to adjust.

If your team is down by a few points or the other team is using a tactic that's working well, don't be afraid to change things up. This could mean switching to a different defensive scheme, being more aggressive on offense, or communicating with your coach to tweak the game plan.

The ability to adapt on the fly is what makes elite athletes stand out. Don't get stuck in one way of thinking—be open to trying new things during the game. Great players shift their strategy based on what the opponent is doing, making them unpredictable and hard to beat.

SECRET #103: MAKE SMART DECISIONS QUICKLY

In fast-paced sports, you don't have time to stop and think about every decision. That's why it's important to practice making quick, smart decisions under pressure.

To improve this skill, work on quick decision-making drills. Set up scenarios that force you to make rapid decisions, like passing the ball while being defended or choosing the right play in a scrimmage. The more you practice, the more instinctive your decision-making will become in real games;

you'll react faster and make better choices in terms of things like knowing when to pass, when to shoot, or when to hold the ball a little longer.

SECRET #104: COMMUNICATE YOUR STRATEGY TO YOUR TEAMMATES

Even the smartest strategy won't work if your teammates don't know what you're thinking. Communication is key to executing any game plan. During a game, make sure you're constantly talking to your teammates—whether it's calling for the ball, letting them know about an open play, or coordinating your movements on defense.

Great teams communicate non-stop during games so that everyone stays on the same page and adjusts the strategy together. Practice communicating in practices, too. The more comfortable you are talking on the field or court, the better you'll be at sharing your strategy during the game.

SECRET #105: STUDY GAME FILM TO IMPROVE YOUR IQ

One of the best ways to boost your game IQ is by watching game film—both your own and others'. Reviewing game footage allows you to see what worked, what didn't, and how you can improve. You can also study your opponents to learn their tendencies and weaknesses. You'll gain a new perspective on the game and spot things you might not notice in the heat of the moment.

When watching your own games, focus on the decisions you made and how they fit into the overall strategy. Did you make the right pass? Were you in the best position? Analyze your performance without the pressure of the game to help you make better decisions next time.

SECRET #106: KNOW WHEN TO BE AGGRESSIVE AND WHEN TO HOLD BACK

A key part of having great game IQ is knowing when to push forward and when to hold back. There are times in every game when you need to be aggressive—taking a shot, going for a steal, or making a bold play. But there are also times when it's smarter to play it safe—passing the ball, maintaining possession, or waiting for a better opportunity.

Learning when to take risks and when to play conservatively is a skill that comes with experience. Pay attention to the flow of the game and trust your instincts. If the game is close or the momentum is on your side, it might be the right time to be aggressive. But if your team is in control or the opponent is pressuring hard, it might be smarter to hold back and play more strategically.

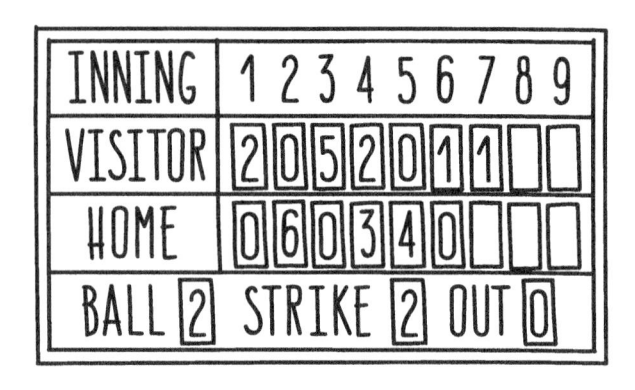

```
┌─────────────────────────────────┐
│ INNING │1 2 3 4 5 6 7 8 9        │
│ VISITOR│[2][0][5][2][0][1][1][ ][ ]│
│ HOME   │[0][6][0][3][4][0][ ][ ][ ]│
│ BALL [2]  STRIKE [2]  OUT [0]   │
└─────────────────────────────────┘
```

SECRET #107: BE AWARE OF TIME AND SCORE SITUATIONS

Understanding the time and score is critical for making smart decisions during a game. If your team is up by a few points with only a minute left, you might want to slow down and protect the ball. But if you're down by a few points with only seconds left, you'll need to push the pace and take more risks.

Great athletes always know how much time is left and what the score is. They use this information to make strategic decisions, like when to call a timeout, when to foul, or when to take a quick shot. Stay aware of the game situation at all times, and use it to guide your actions.

SECRET #108: MASTER THE ART OF DECEPTION

Deception is a powerful tool in sports. If your opponent knows exactly what you're going to do, it's easy for them to stop you. But if you can keep them guessing, you'll be much harder to defend. Deception comes in many forms—for example, faking a pass, using your eyes to mislead a defender, or pretending to take a shot before making a move.

Practice the art of deception in your games. Learn how to fake out defenders and create opportunities by making them think you're going one way when you're really going another. The more unpredictable you are, the more successful you'll be.

SECRET #109: TRUST YOUR INSTINCTS

Ultimately, strategy and game IQ come down to trusting your instincts. You've put in the work during practice, studied your opponents, and learned the strategies—now it's time to trust yourself. In the heat of the game, there's no time for second-guessing. Rely on your instincts and make quick decisions with confidence.

The more you practice, the sharper your instincts will become. Great athletes know that trusting their gut in high-pressure situations often leads to the best outcomes. So, when it's time to make a play, go with your instincts and play fearlessly.

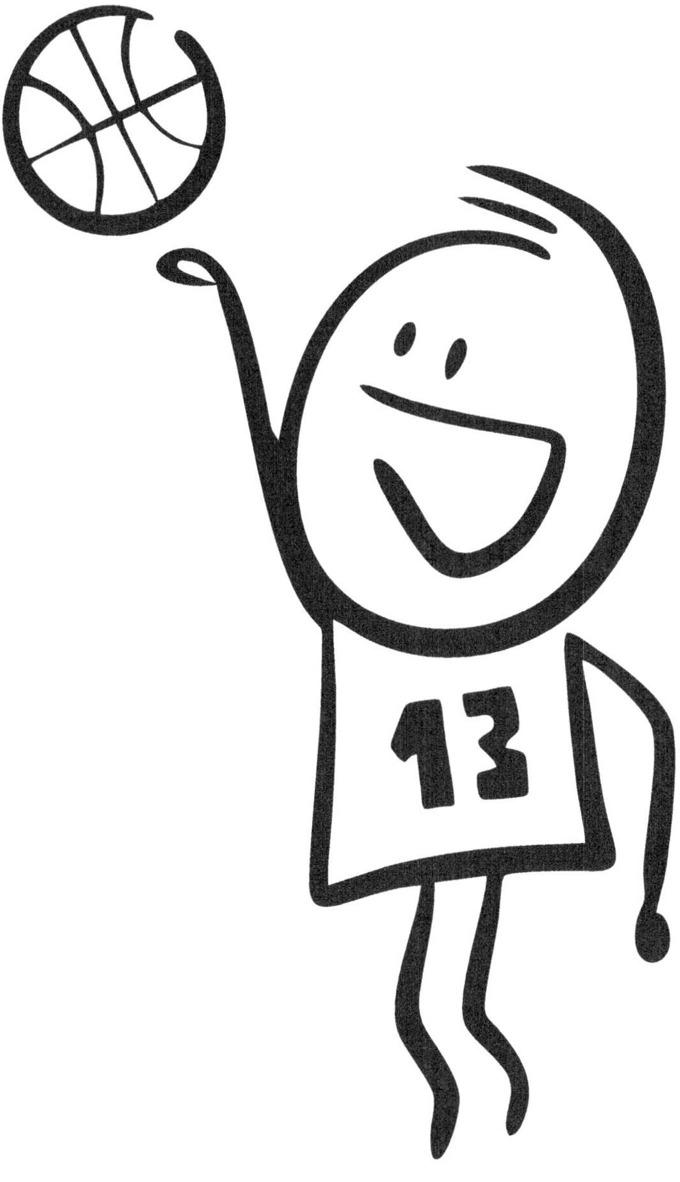
13

Chapter 10
COMPETITION AND RIVALRIES

Competition is a natural part of sports, and while it can push you to be better, it can also bring challenges, like having to deal with pressure and manage rivalries. Learning how to handle competition in a healthy and productive way is key to staying focused and becoming the best athlete you can be. This chapter will give you the tools to manage competition, stay motivated, and keep rivalries positive.

SECRET #110: KEEP RIVALRIES HEALTHY

Rivalries are common in sports, but they don't have to be negative. In fact, a healthy rivalry can push you to work harder and improve your skills. The key to keeping rivalries positive is respect. Even if you're competing fiercely, always show respect for your opponent's effort and abilities.

Avoid trash talk or negative behavior, which can lead to toxic and unnecessary conflict. Instead, focus on pushing yourself to be better and let your performance speak for itself. After the competition, show good sportsmanship by congratulating your rival on a good game. Healthy rivalries motivate you to improve while keeping the spirit of competition respectful and productive.

SECRET #111: STAY FOCUSED ON YOUR OWN PERFORMANCE

It's easy to get caught up in what your competitors are doing, but the best athletes stay focused on their own performance. Constantly comparing yourself to others can make you feel discouraged or anxious, especially if they're performing better than you. Instead of focusing on what others are doing, keep your attention on your own goals and how you can improve.

When you're in a competition, remind yourself that the only thing you can control is your own effort. Stay focused on your own performance so you can give your best effort and make smarter decisions during the game. Remember, the best athletes focus on their own growth rather than worrying about everyone else.

SECRET #112: LEARN HOW TO HANDLE PRESSURE

With competition comes pressure, which can cause you to make mistakes, lose focus, or feel overwhelmed. Learning how to handle that pressure is a crucial part of being a successful athlete.

One technique is to take deep breaths and focus on the present moment. When you're feeling the pressure, slow your breathing and bring your attention to what's happening right now rather than worrying about the outcome.

Another way to handle pressure is to remind yourself that it's okay to make mistakes. No athlete is perfect; everyone makes errors, especially in high-pressure situations. The key is to stay calm, refocus, and keep playing your game. This will enable you to perform at your best, even in the most intense situations.

SECRET #113: COMPETE AGAINST YOURSELF, NOT JUST OTHERS

While it's natural to compete against others, the most important competition is the one you have with yourself. Focus on becoming better than you were yesterday rather than just trying to beat someone else. Set personal goals for improvement, whether it's running faster, improving your technique, or mastering a new skill.

Competing against yourself puts the control of your progress and growth in your hands. Even if you don't win every competition, you'll still feel proud of the improvements you've made. The more you focus on your own development, the more fulfilling your athletic journey will be.

SECRET #114: STAY HUMBLE IN VICTORY, GRACIOUS IN DEFEAT

How you handle both victory and defeat says a lot about your character as an athlete. When you win, it's important to stay humble and avoid boasting or rubbing it in your opponent's face. Show respect for your competitor's effort and recognize that every victory is a result of hard work and teamwork.

When you lose, be gracious. Congratulate your opponent and reflect on what you can learn from the experience. Defeat is an important part of sports because it teaches you resilience and how to improve. By staying humble in victory and gracious in defeat, you'll earn respect from your teammates, coaches, and competitors.

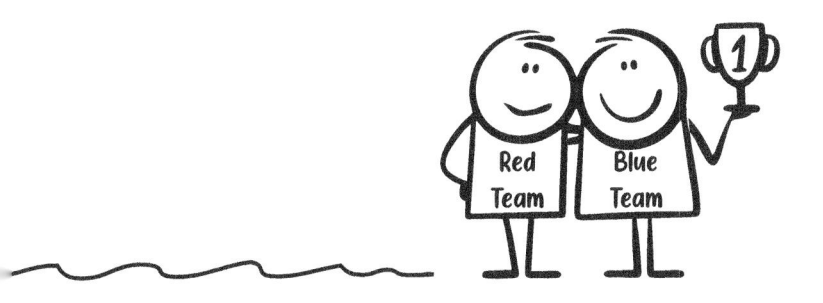

SECRET #115: RESPECT YOUR COMPETITORS

It's easy to think of your competitors as "the enemy," but in reality, they're helping you grow as an athlete. Without competition, you wouldn't have the opportunity to push your limits and test your skills. Show respect for your competitors by recognizing their effort and dedication. This creates an atmosphere of mutual respect and sportsmanship.

This doesn't mean you should be any less competitive—in fact, you'll compete even harder, knowing that your opponent is doing the same. At the end of the day, competition is about bringing out the best in both you and your opponents.

SECRET #116: CHANNEL NERVOUS ENERGY INTO FOCUS

It's natural to feel nervous before a big game or competition, but that nervous energy can actually be a good thing if you know how to channel it. Instead of letting nerves make you feel anxious or shaky, use them to sharpen your focus. Nervous energy is just your body's way of getting ready to perform, so embrace it as part of the process.

When you feel nervous, take deep breaths and remind yourself that it's a sign that you care about doing well. Use that energy to focus on your strategy, stay present in the moment, and play with intensity. This will help you feel more confident and prepared in high-pressure situations.

If you apply these secrets, you'll be better equipped to handle competition in a healthy, productive way. You'll develop the mental strength needed to face tough competitors, build resilience, and stay motivated while keeping rivalries respectful and positive.

Chapter 11
BUILDING SPEED, AGILITY, AND STRENGTH

Speed, agility, and strength are key components of success in almost any sport. Whether you're running down the field, dodging opponents, or powering through a tough play, these physical skills give you the edge you need. In this chapter, we'll explore how to improve in each of these three skills to become a more powerful and versatile athlete.

SECRET #117: FOCUS ON SPRINT TRAINING TO IMPROVE SPEED

If you want to get faster, sprint training should be a key part of your routine. Sprinting helps you develop explosive speed, which is critical for short bursts of movement during a game—whether it's chasing down a ball, sprinting to the finish line, or breaking away from an opponent.

To improve your sprinting, focus on short, intense bursts of speed. Start with 20- to 30-meter sprints, and gradually increase the distance as you get faster. Make sure to rest between sprints so you can give your maximum effort on each one. As you practice, pay attention to your form—keep your body upright, pump your arms, and push off the ground with power. Sprinting regularly will help you build the speed you need to outpace your opponents.

SECRET #118: BUILD EXPLOSIVE POWER WITH PLYOMETRIC EXERCISES

Plyometric exercises, also known as "jump training," are designed to build explosive power, which is essential for speed and agility. These exercises involve quick, powerful movements that help your muscles generate force rapidly—just like you need to do in sports. Plyometrics improve your ability to jump higher, move faster, and change direction quickly.

Some effective plyometric exercises include box jumps, jump squats, and lateral bounds. Start with low repetitions and focus on quality over quantity—perform each jump with as much power and control as possible. As you get stronger, you can increase the height of your jumps or add more complex movements. Plyometric training will not only make you more explosive but also improve your coordination and balance.

SECRET #119: INCORPORATE AGILITY DRILLS INTO YOUR TRAINING

Agility is all about how quickly and efficiently you can change direction without losing speed or control. In many sports, being agile allows you to dodge defenders, react to fast-paced plays, and maintain your balance during quick movements. To improve your agility, practice drills that require you to change direction quickly and frequently.

One common agility exercise is the cone drill, where you set up cones in a pattern and run or shuffle between them. You can also practice ladder drills, where you move your feet quickly through the spaces of a speed ladder laid on the ground. Agility drills improve your footwork, balance, and coordination, helping you become a more nimble and responsive athlete.

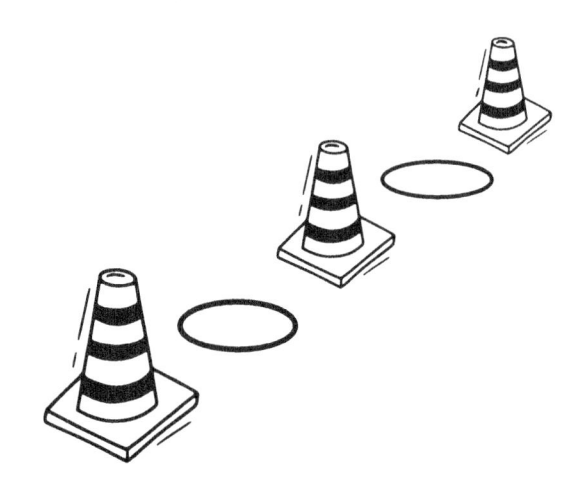

SECRET #120: STRENGTHEN YOUR CORE FOR STABILITY AND POWER

Your core muscles—those in your abdomen, lower back, and hips—are the foundation of your strength, stability, and balance. A strong core helps you maintain control during fast movements, improves your balance when changing direction, and enhances your overall power. If your core is weak, you'll be more prone to injury and won't perform at your full potential.

To strengthen your core, include exercises like planks, Russian twists, and leg raises in your training routine. Focus on engaging your core during every exercise to get the most out of your workout. A strong core will make you more stable and powerful, whether you're sprinting, jumping, or defending against an opponent.

SECRET #121: BUILD LOWER BODY STRENGTH FOR SPEED AND POWER

Your lower body—legs, glutes, and hips—provides the foundation for both speed and power. Building strength in these muscles will help you run faster, jump higher, and move with better control. Squats, lunges, and deadlifts are some of the best exercises for developing lower body strength.

When performing these exercises, focus on proper form to prevent injury and maximize your gains. As you get stronger, you can add weights to increase the challenge.

Strong legs and glutes are essential for any athlete looking to improve their speed, power, and agility on the field or court.

SECRET #122: WORK ON FLEXIBILITY FOR BETTER MOVEMENT AND INJURY PREVENTION

Flexibility is often overlooked, but it plays a crucial role in speed, agility, and injury prevention. Flexible muscles and joints allow you to move more freely and efficiently, which also reduces the risk of muscle strains and other injuries.

Incorporate stretching into your daily routine, especially after workouts when your muscles are warm. Focus on stretches that target the muscles used in your sport, such as your hamstrings, quads, calves, and hip flexors. Dynamic stretches, like leg swings and arm circles, are great for warming up before a game, while static stretches help improve flexibility after your workout.

SECRET #123: TRAIN WITH RESISTANCE BANDS FOR EXPLOSIVE STRENGTH

Resistance bands are a versatile tool that can help you build explosive strength without needing heavy weights. These bands provide variable resistance, meaning they get harder to stretch the more you pull, which mimics the resistance your muscles face during the dynamic movements required in sports. Using resistance bands during your training helps improve your strength, speed, and agility all at once.

Use resistance bands to train your legs by performing banded squats, leg presses, or hip extensions, or use them for upper body exercises like rows and presses to build strength in your arms, shoulders, and back.

SECRET #124: IMPROVE REACTION TIME WITH REACTION DRILLS

Speed and agility aren't just about how fast you can move—they're also about how quickly you can react to a situation. Improving your reaction time helps you respond faster to opponents, make quicker decisions, and stay ahead of the competition. Reaction drills are designed to improve this aspect of your game by training your brain to respond faster to stimuli.

One simple reaction drill is to have a partner throw a ball in different directions, and you must catch or deflect it as quickly as possible. You can also use agility drills, like sprinting when a coach blows a whistle or reacting to visual cues. The more you practice reacting quickly, the faster your brain and body will be able to respond during a game.

SECRET #125: BUILD UPPER BODY STRENGTH FOR POWER AND STABILITY

While speed and agility are a big focus, having a strong upper body is just as important for maintaining balance, power, and control. Whether you're pushing through an opponent, making a quick pass, or using your arms to drive forward in a sprint, upper body strength plays a key role in your overall athleticism.

To build upper body strength, incorporate exercises like push-ups, pull-ups, and bench presses into your training. Don't forget to include shoulder exercises like overhead presses and rows, as strong shoulders help stabilize your upper body during dynamic movements. A balanced upper body strengthens your entire game and enhances your speed and agility.

SECRET #126: FOCUS ON RECOVERY TO MAINTAIN YOUR GAINS

As you work on building speed, agility, and strength, make sure not to overlook recovery. Training hard without giving your body time to recover can lead to burnout, fatigue, and injury, which will slow down your progress. Schedule rest days into your routine and give your muscles time to repair and grow stronger.

In addition, active recovery, like light jogging, stretching, or yoga, can help keep your muscles loose and reduce soreness. Proper sleep, hydration, and nutrition also play a key role in recovery, so be sure to take care of your body off the field as well. A well-rounded recovery routine helps you maintain your gains and come back stronger for every practice and game.

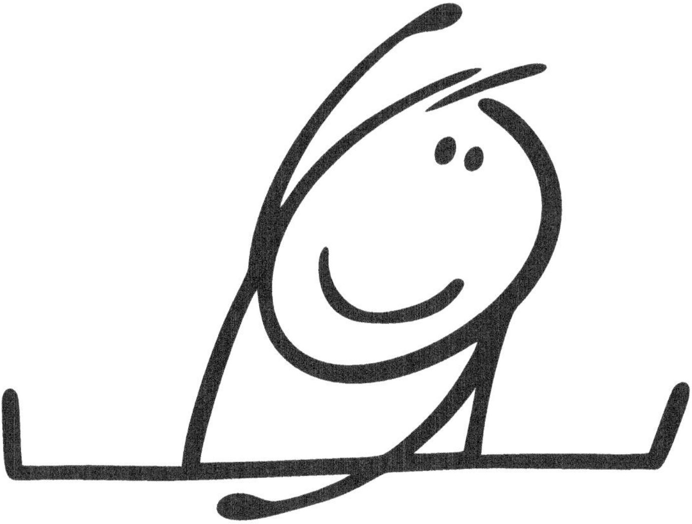

Chapter 12
GAME DAY PREPARATION

Game day is the moment you've been training for, but showing up ready to play goes beyond just physical preparation. Preparing mentally, emotionally, and physically can make all the difference in how you perform. In this chapter, we'll explore the secrets to preparing for game day so you can step onto the field or court with confidence and perform at your best.

SECRET #127: GET ENOUGH REST THE NIGHT BEFORE

One of the most important things you can do to prepare for game day is to get a good night's sleep. Sleep is essential for your body to recover and recharge, and it ensures that you're mentally sharp and physically ready to perform. Aim for at least 8-10 hours of sleep the night before your game, and create a relaxing bedtime routine to help you wind down.

Avoid staying up late or using screens (like phones or tablets) before bed, as this can interfere with your sleep quality. Good sleep hygiene—like sleeping in a dark, quiet room and keeping a consistent bedtime—will help ensure you wake up feeling rested and ready to play.

SECRET #128: FUEL YOUR BODY WITH A HEALTHY PRE-GAME MEAL

What you eat before a game has a big impact on your performance. Your body needs fuel in the form of carbohydrates, protein, and healthy fats to give you the energy and endurance you need. About 3-4 hours before your game, eat a balanced meal that includes foods like whole grains (oatmeal, rice, or pasta), lean proteins (chicken, fish, or eggs), and healthy fats (avocado or nuts).

Avoid heavy or greasy foods, which can make you feel sluggish or upset your stomach. Hydration is just as important, so make sure you're drinking water throughout the day to stay hydrated. A well-fueled body is one that can perform at its peak and stay strong throughout the game.

SECRET #129: VISUALIZE SUCCESS BEFORE THE GAME STARTS

Mental preparation is just as important as physical preparation. Before your game, take some time to sit quietly and visualize yourself performing well. Imagine yourself making successful plays, staying calm under pressure, and helping your team win. Visualization primes your brain for success, so when you're actually in the game, you'll feel more confident and prepared.

Visualization also helps you manage pre-game nerves. Instead of feeling anxious, you'll feel more in control and focused on what you need to do. The more you practice visualization, the better you'll get at mentally preparing yourself for game day.

SECRET #130: CREATE A PRE-GAME ROUTINE

Having a consistent pre-game routine helps with mental and physical preparation. This routine can include things like eating a light snack, listening to music that pumps you up, doing a few stretches, or going over the game plan with your coach or teammates to get into the right mindset and feel more focused and ready to play.

The key is to find what works best for you. Some athletes prefer quiet time to mentally prepare, while others like to get hyped up with music or team chants. Whatever your routine is, stick with it so it becomes a part of your game day ritual.

SECRET #131: STAY HYDRATED DURING THE GAME

Proper hydration doesn't stop when the game starts—you need to keep drinking water throughout the game to maintain your energy levels and avoid cramping. Dehydration can lead to fatigue, dizziness, and muscle cramps, all of which will negatively impact your performance.

During the game, take advantage of any breaks to drink water. If the game is particularly long or you're playing in hot weather, consider drinking a sports drink with electrolytes to help replace what you've lost through sweat. Staying hydrated keeps your muscles working efficiently and helps you stay focused and alert on the field.

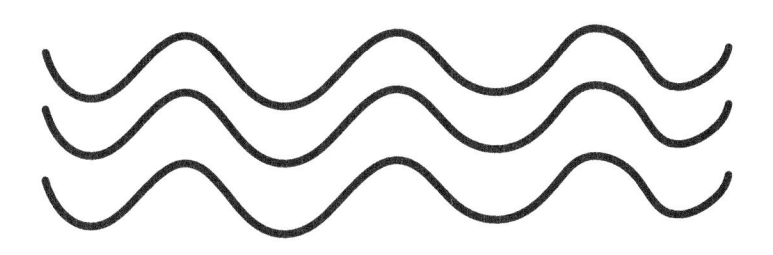

SECRET #132: DO A PROPER WARM-UP BEFORE THE GAME

Warming up before a game is essential for getting your body ready to perform. A proper warm-up increases your heart rate, warms up your muscles, and prepares your joints for the physical demands of the game. Skipping your warm-up or doing it too quickly can increase your risk of injury and slow down your performance.

A good warm-up should include dynamic stretches, light cardio, and sport-specific movements. For example, if you play soccer, you might do some light jogging, leg swings, and dribbling drills. The goal is to gradually raise your heart rate and get your body ready for high-intensity movements. This will help you start the game feeling loose, focused, and energized.

SECRET #133: REVIEW YOUR STRATEGY AND GAME PLAN

Going into the game with a clear understanding of your strategy will help you stay focused and make smart decisions. Before the game starts, review the game plan with your coach and teammates. Make sure everyone understands their roles and responsibilities, as well as the team's overall strategy.

Knowing the game plan inside and out will give you confidence and help you make quicker decisions during the game. It also helps you stay flexible—if things aren't going as planned, you'll be able to adapt and make adjustments with your team.

SECRET #134: PACE YOURSELF THROUGHOUT THE GAME

While it's tempting to go all-out from the start, you need to pace yourself so you have energy left for the entire game. Start strong, but avoid burning all your energy in the first half. Instead, focus on maintaining a steady level of effort so you can push harder when it counts most—toward the end of the game.

Pay attention to how your body feels during the game and adjust accordingly. Take advantage of breaks to catch your breath, rehydrate, and refocus. Pacing yourself will help you stay strong and finish the game with energy and intensity.

Time to hydrate!

CONCLUSION

Congratulations on reaching the end of *Everything Young Athletes Need to Know!* By reading through these secrets, you've taken an important step toward becoming not only a better athlete but also a stronger, more confident person. The journey you're on—whether it's in sports or life—will be filled with challenges, victories, and lessons. The most important thing to remember is that growth doesn't happen overnight. It's a process that requires dedication, patience, and a positive mindset.

The lessons you've learned in this book are just the beginning of your journey. As you continue to train, compete, and grow, remember that success is a marathon, not a sprint. Stay patient, stay focused, and always look for new ways to improve.

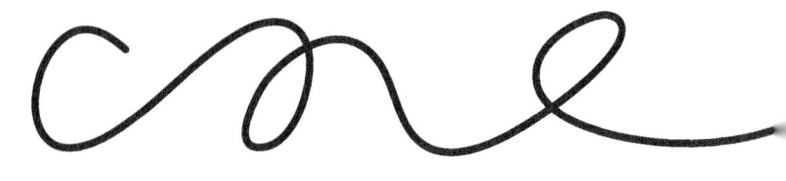

Whether you're chasing big dreams in sports or pursuing other goals in life, the principles you've learned here—hard work, perseverance, and a positive mindset—will guide you to success.

So go out there, keep pushing your limits, and never stop believing in your potential. Your journey is yours to shape, and the future is full of opportunities for you to shine. Good luck and enjoy every step of the way!

LEAVE YOUR FEEDBACK ON AMAZON

Please think about leaving some feedback via a review on Amazon.

It may only take a moment, but it really does mean the world for small publishers like us :)

PARENTS, DON'T FORGET YOUR
FREE GIFTS!

Simply visit

haydenfoxmedia.com

to receive the following:

1000 Conversation Starters
the Whole Family Will Love

100 Fun Screen-Free Activity Ideas
to Enjoy Together as a Family

(You can also scan this QR code)

MORE TITLES WE ARE SURE YOU WILL LOVE!

Printed in Great Britain
by Amazon